Eva Meets her Inner Team

A story about meeting all the parts of you

Written by Rebecca Halstead

Copyright © 2025 by Rebecca Halstead

All rights reserved. No part of this publication may be reproduced, distributed, or transmitted in any form or by any means, including photocopying, recording, or other electronic or mechanical methods, without the prior written permission of the publisher, except in the case of brief quotations embodied in critical reviews and certain other noncommercial uses permitted by copyright law.

This book draws on psychological frameworks but is intended for educational purposes only.

This book is a Growth Circuit™ product, you can find us at www.thegrowthcircuit.com

For permissions, contact: hello@thegrowthcircuit.com

ISBN: 978-1-7642913-0-9 (paperback)
ISBN: 978-1-7642913-1-6 (hardcover)

Contents

Chapter 1 – The Shaky Show and Tell 1

Chapter 2 – Meeting the Inner Team 5

Chapter 3 – Mirror Talk Magic 10

Chapter 4 – Curious Questions 15

Chapter 5 – Nala's Worries 22

Chapter 6 – Team Celebration 28

Chapter 7 – Thank You, Inner Team 30

Chapter 1: The Shaky Show & Tell

Eva's heart was doing somersaults.

Today was show and tell, and her fingers clung to her backpack straps.

Inside was Poppy's old blue guitar, the one he played every Sunday morning.

She wanted to show it. She really did! But her belly buzzed with bees, not butterflies, but bees.

Mrs Clover smiled at the front of the room. "Eva, sweetheart, you're up next."

Eva's legs turned to jelly. Her hands got sweaty. She didn't move.

Then it started. That voice.

What if your hands shake? What if you drop the guitar and it breaks? What if everyone laughs at you?

The voice pressed down on her thoughts, heavy and hard.

Just stay seated, it whispered. *Better safe than sorry.*

Eva glanced at her best friend, William, in his wheelchair. "You've got this," he mouthed.

She managed a half-smile. But her legs still wouldn't move.

And then… something strange happened.

Next to her pencil case, a shimmer glowed. She blinked. No one else noticed. It floated up and pop!

That's when Eva saw something she couldn't explain. Something small. Something magical. Something that would change her forever.

Because today, Eva wasn't just going to face her fear. She was going to meet her **INNER TEAM.**

Chapter 2: Meeting the Inner Team

Where the shimmer had popped, a tiny person now stood on Eva's desk. Brown hair, sneakers with stars, and a grin as wide as his face.

"Name's Confident Charlie. I live inside you."

Eva blinked. "Inside me?"

"Yep. I'm the part that knows you can do hard things, like playing Poppy's guitar with courage and confidence."

"I don't feel brave," she whispered. Charlie tilted his head. "Because she's been talking again."

He pointed toward the shadow under Eva's desk. Out stepped a girl with crossed arms and stormy eyes.

That's Negative Nala," Charlie said. "She thinks she's helping, but really, she just shouts 'what ifs' until you forget how strong you are."

"I *am* helping," Nala snapped. "Someone has to stop Eva from looking silly."

Eva shivered. This was so strange… and kind of amazing.

Before she could speak, a voice squeaked, *HELLOOOO!"*

Sliding down her pencil came a girl in a polka-dot lab coat, magnifying glass in hand.

"I'm Curious Candice! I ask, I explore, I try! I think, what if you play your guitar and people LOVE it?"

From behind the eraser, a calm smile appeared. ***"I'm Thoughtful Thelma,*** I notice how you breathe when you're scared, and how proud you feel when you're brave."

Then another voice called out, ***"I'm Caring Claire!*** I help you with kindness, to yourself, to others, and even to the planet!"

Eva's eyebrows lifted. "There's… a team inside me?"

"Yep," said Charlie. "We're your Inner Team. We help you choose what to do when thoughts and feelings get loud."

Nala hugged herself tighter. "I just don't want her to fall apart."

Charlie's voice softened.

"We get it, Nala. But fear doesn't get to be the boss."

Eva let out a shaky breath. She didn't feel totally brave, but she felt different. Not alone.

"So," Charlie said with a grin, "want to learn a trick to feel braver, even when your legs feel like jelly?"

Eva nodded. She was ready.

Chapter 3: Mirror Talk Magic

Eva followed Charlie's tiny footsteps across her desk. He stopped at her water bottle and pointed to the shiny surface.

"See that?" he said. "Your reflection is the tool."

Eva leaned closer. Her face looked nervous… eyes wide, lips tight.

"That's the face of a girl who cares," said Charlie. "She's scared because this matters."

Eva tilted her head. "So, what do I do with the reflection or mirror?"

Charlie grinned and pulled out a little gold card.

It read: ***MIRROR TALK MAGIC!!***

Say it. See it. Believe it.

You stand in front of something shiny and speak words that help the real you sound louder than Nala."

"Isn't that just like talking to myself?" Eva asked.

"Exactly," said Charlie. "On purpose, with power."

He struck a superhero pose. "Try this one: *I can do brave things, even when I feel wobbly.*"

Eva whispered it once.

"Say it like you mean it," Charlie urged. "Like you'd say it to William if he was nervous."

Eva stood taller. "I can do brave things… even when I feel wobbly."

A small smile flickered.

"Each time," Charlie said, "make your voice stronger."

Eva didn't feel fearless, but something inside her stretched, like she was growing.

She whispered, "I can imagine myself strumming the guitar."

Charlie nodded. "That's a great start. **Say it. See it. Believe it.**"

Miss Clover's voice brought Eva back. "Eva? Are you ready now, love?"

The room was quiet. Everyone was watching.

Eva swallowed. Charlie gave her a nod. William's thumbs up made her chest warm.

Eva stood. Slowly. Carefully. *I can do brave things,* she thought.

And she took her first step to the front of the class, guitar in hand, Inner Team by her side.

Chapter 4: Curious Questions

Eva stood at the front of the classroom, her guitar resting gently across her body.

She picked it up, breathed in… and let out a long breath. She strummed softly.

Plink… plonk… pling. The strings buzzed. Her fingers shook.

This was a bad idea, she thought.

Everyone's going to stare. What if I cry? What if I freeze?

Negative Nala paced behind her pencil case, arms folded, storm cloud over her head. "You're not ready. You'll mess up. They'll laugh."

Eva's chest grew tight. The thoughts were hot, like lava.

Confident Charlie hopped beside her. "Nala's tossing out ***Volcano Thoughts*** again."

"Volcano thoughts?" Eva asked.

"Yep. They explode in your brain and make everything feel worse."

"Like… *Everyone will laugh at me?*

"Exactly. Hot and scary, but not the whole truth."

Thoughtful Thelma peeked up from behind a dictionary. "They're often *what ifs,* like *what if I fail?*

Thelma added, "You have to ask yourself… is this thought helpful, or just a volcano trying to erupt?"

Eva nodded slowly and said,

"What if I drop the guitar? What if my voice shakes? What if I forget everything?"

"Those are Volcano Thoughts," Thelma said gently.

"Let's find a **Rainbow Thought** instead."

Eva frowned. "What's a **Rainbow Thought?**"

Charlie leaned closer. "It's a thought that's kind and helpful. It still sees clouds but looks for colours too."

Eva tried one.

Volcano: *Everyone will laugh at me.*

Rainbow: *Some might not care… but some might smile, and I'll be proud I tried.*

Suddenly a messy-haired boy in a backwards cap shouted, "JUST GO FOR IT! SMASH IT!"

Eva jumped. "Who are you?!"

"I'm Impulsive Isaac!" he grinned. "I'm the DO IT NOW part. Forget the plan, just MOVE!"

Charlie laughed. "Isaac means well, but he skips the thinking part."

Thelma raised her hand. "Sometimes it's brave to pause. Just for a breath."

Eva smiled. Isaac's energy was fun, but too fast for now. "I like that you believe in me," she said. "But I need one more deep breath."

Isaac saluted, then backflipped away.

Eva looked at her Inner Team. She strummed again, stronger this time.

Nala was quieter now. Isaac bounced in the corner. Thelma nodded. Charlie fist pumped. Candice smiled brightly, Claire blew a kiss.

And William smiled, the kind of smile that said, *I believe in you*.

"I can do brave things," Eva whispered. And this time, she believed it.

She lifted her guitar with both hands, her team inside her, and one very big ***Rainbow Thought*** in her head.

21

Chapter 5: Nala's Worries

The classroom felt different as Eva stood in front of her class.

Not quieter. Not louder. Just… sharper, like the colours were brighter and the air lighter.

Her knees felt floaty, like jelly on a trampoline. But she didn't sit down.

Miss Clover smiled. "Eva, whenever you're ready."

Eva took a deep breath.

Her fingers shook as she adjusted the guitar. She placed one hand on the strings… and paused.

"Don't mess it up," whispered Negative Nala.

Eva turned her head slightly.

"It's okay, Nala," she whispered back. "I know you're trying to protect me. But I've got this."

Behind her ear, Charlie gave a small cheer. "That's what I'm talking about."

Thelma's gentle voice followed. "Deep breath… just play the first note."

From behind her lunchbox, Isaac bounced like a yo-yo. "Do it! Just go!"

Eva nodded. To all of them. She strummed.

The first note wobbled. The second was steadier.

By the third, something opened in her chest, like a window letting in sunlight.

The bees in her belly softened into butterflies, just the right kind of flutter.

She began to play the tune her Poppy had taught her, the one he wrote when her mum was born.

It was soft. Simple. Beautiful.

Her classmates sat still, listening. Eva didn't look at their faces. She didn't need to.

She looked at the guitar, at her hands…and noticed the feeling blooming inside her chest.

When the last note rang out, the room was silent. One… two… three seconds.

Then came the applause.

Not loud. Not wild. Just warm, like a hug made of claps.

Miss Clover smiled. "Thank you, Eva. That was really special."

Eva smiled too.

Not because it was perfect, because it wasn't. She missed a note. Her hand slipped. Her foot tapped too fast..

But she had stood tall, even when she felt unsure and scared.

And that was more than enough.

Chapter 6: Team Celebration

After show and tell, Eva and William sat on the hill outside the library, sharing apple slices and stories.

"You were awesome," William said. "That guitar song gave me goosebumps."

Eva laughed. "My fingers were shaking the whole time."

"Still played it though," he said. "That's what counts."

Eva leaned back in the grass and looked up at the clouds. They drifted lazily across the sky, soft and light, like her thoughts.

"You know what's weird?" she said. "I have this whole team inside me. They talk. They help. Sometimes they get in each other's way."

William grinned. "Sounds like a superhero squad."

"Kind of," Eva smiled. "Only… they're all me."

Chapter 7: Thank You, Inner Team

That night, after brushing her teeth, Eva stood in front of the mirror. Her reflection stared back… a little braver, a little taller.

One by one, her Inner Team appeared around the glass:

Charlie, beaming. Candice, eyes sparkling. Thelma, calm in her prayer pose. Isaac, bouncing on his toes. Nala, quiet in the corner. Claire, making a love-heart with her hands.

Eva turned to them. "You all helped today. Even you, Nala."

Nala blinked. "Me?"

"You reminded me to be careful. You were scared because you didn't want me to mess up."

Nala gave a small smile. "I guess I did try."

Eva nodded. "And Isaac, I'm sorry I didn't listen right away."

"That's okay!" Isaac grinned. "I'm great for jump-in moments."

Eva laughed. "You're all important, I just need different ones of you at different times."

Thelma stepped forward. "It's not just who shows up. It's when. Timing matters."

Eva thought about it. Sometimes I need to pause. Sometimes I need to act. Sometimes I need to wonder. And sometimes…I need to feel scared and keep going.

She looked at her reflection, her Inner Team smiling behind her.

"Thanks, team," she whispered.

Together, they faded into the glow of the mirror, not gone, just quieter now, waiting for the next time she needed them.

Knowing her Inner Team was there, made Eva feel more confident and self-aware....*And that changed everything.*

Author's Note: A Message for Parents

Eva Meets Her Inner Team is more than a story. It is a playful introduction to skills that help children build emotional intelligence. The characters and dialogue are inspired by evidence-based practices like Cognitive Behaviour Therapy (CBT), and Polyvagal Theory, parts works. These ideas have been simplified for children, but they remain powerful when practiced regularly, especially with the support of trusted adults.

Through this story, children learn to reduce shame and fear by giving their big feelings a voice through playful characters. They are introduced to tools such as Mirror Talk Magic, Volcano and Rainbow Thoughts, and compassionate self-talk. They also see how to talk back to negative self-talk, pause before acting, reframe anxious thinking, and choose courage over perfection.

The affirmations in italics, like *I can do brave things*, are designed to be read aloud or used as mirror work. They show children how to strengthen positive inner voices while reminding them that all parts of themselves have a place, even the scared or impulsive ones. Fear doesn't have to be the boss.

You can use this book as a springboard for conversations about emotions, choices, and self-compassion. The bolded phrases highlight psychological tools that you can return to with your child in everyday life. You don't need to explain everything at once. Simply start noticing when a part, like Nala or Isaac, shows up.

This book is not only about Eva's Inner Team. It is an invitation for your child to begin recognizing their own inner team. With that awareness, they can grow into themselves with courage, curiosity, kindness, and care.